SUPER STYLE

SUPER STYLE

Written by Carol Spier

Photography by Angela Coppola

LONDON, NEW YORK, MUNICH,
MELBOURNE AND DELHI

Editor Elizabeth Hester
Senior Designer Tai Blanche
Managing Art Editor Michelle Baxter
Art Director Dirk Kaufman
Publishing Director Beth Sutinis
Lead Illustrator Jeremy Canceko
Additional Illustrations Matt Dicke,
Paul Hoppe, Engly Cheng, Erin Harney
Production Ivor Parker
DTP Design Kathy Farias

DOWNTOWN
BOOKWORKS INC.

Produced by Downtown Bookworks Inc.
President: Julie Merberg
Director: Patty Brown
Editor: Sarah Parvis

Photographer Angela Coppola
Freelance Beauty Editor JoanneNoel Higgins

First published in the United States in 2006 by
DK Publishing, Inc.
375 Hudson Street, New York, NY 10014

06 07 08 09 10 10 9 8 7 6 5 4 3 2 1

Library of Congress Cataloging-in-Publication Data
Spier, Carol.
super style / written by Carol Spier.-- 1st American ed.
p. cm.
Includes index.
ISBN 0-7566-1588-7 (pbk.)
1. Dress accessories. 2. Fashion.
TT560.S65 2006
646'.308352--dc22
2005031583

Color reproduction by Colourscan, Singapore
Printed and bound in Mexico by
R. R. Donnelley and Sons Co.

Discover more at
www.dk.com

Contents

Get Ready to Show Your Style

Choose Jewelry That's Perfect for You

Pick the Pieces that Tie Your Look Together

Who Will You Be Today?

Nierah

Alexis

Amy

Nikki

Rosie

Get ready to show your style

Fashion accessories (and knowing how to use them effectively) can totally transform the most basic T-shirt and jeans into a look loaded with style. Style is often about the details—like what shape, color, and material something is made of, what kind of motif (like a flower or stripes) it features, and what scale it is (very big, very small, or in between). The way these details are combined can create a specific look, like preppy or glam. Or the style can speak volumes about the girl who puts it together. No matter what you choose, you create an expression of your personal style every time you get dressed. So make sure your look includes lots of personality, lots of fun, and lots of *you*!

Style 101

What is style? It can be a look that you see in a book, in a magazine, or on TV and then recreate on yourself. Or style can be original—something that you create on your own. You can change your style often, or pick one as a signature look. Just remember these two style basics as you explore: 1) Remember that less is usually more—don't wear it all at once, even if you love it. 2) Trust your instincts—if you like the way you look, you'll communicate self-confidence!

Look at you!

What's your best look? For clues, look in the mirror. Your own features can help you find a style that's totally unique—and totally flattering. Note your coloring and face shape, then watch for these icons in the book for cool style tips just for you!

Round faces like Amy's have wide cheeks and equal curves—as if the bridge of the nose is the center of a circle. Amy also considers her light hair when picking out accessories—dark earrings really stand out.

Heart-shaped faces are widest across the forehead, with a narrow chin—like an upside down triangle. Nikki likes to balance this shape with eye-catching earrings.

Oval faces curve pretty equally above and below the cheeks, but the face is longer than it is wide. Rosie's olive-toned skin and brown hair make gold-toned jewelry a great choice for her.

Alexis has a square face, which is of nearly equal width at the forehead and jawline. With her fair, pinkish skin, she looks for rosy accessories to match.

Like Amy, Nierah has a round face. With her shorter hair, it's easy for her to draw attention to her favorite necklaces and scarves. She can also play up her dark skin with warm gold tones or bold colors.

Find your face shape

Have you ever noticed how the same pair of sunglasses can look amazing on one girl and silly on another? It's all about face shape. Learning to complement yours can help you find styles that are always flattering. Use this trick to find your shape, then have fun finding the best looks for you.

1 Hold your head still as you look in the mirror. Using a china marker, an inexpensive lipstick, or a bar of soap, make dots at the highest, lowest, and widest points of your reflection.

2 Next, connect the dots with lines that follow your hair- and jawlines. The result is a flattened version of your face shape.

School

Wear just a few informal accessories to school; keep everything small except for your book bag and maybe your watch.

Shopping

Fun, colorful things are great for hanging out with your friends or shopping. Choose a small shoulder bag to keep your hands free.

What to wear when

Accessories are attention-grabbers. Part of being stylish is knowing how to dress for different events and places. Here's a rule of thumb to help you decide: A little of anything goes almost anywhere, but a lot of it goes only certain places. For example, rhinestone studs can go to school, but rhinestone chandelier earrings should not!

Out to dinner

Go for a pulled together look with a belt
and some jewelry to dress up simple clothes.
Carry a bag to hold your grooming gear.

Fancy party

Glittery and shiny things are perfect for
special parties and weddings. Don't overdo
it—a few pretty things are all you need.

Choose jewelry that's perfect for you

If you love necklaces, earrings, bracelets, and rings, you've got the jewelry bug! Jewelry is a great way to finish off an outfit, add lots of personality to a look, and make your face and hands look pretty. You can totally change the look of an outfit by changing the jewelry you wear with it. In this section, we'll show what you should be thinking about when you approach your jewelry box. Are you headed to a game, or out to dinner? Do you want to go for a specific look, or try something completely new? What colors and textures does your outfit have? Once you see how to choose the pieces that are right for you, you'll be ready to step out in style!

Studs & drops are simply stylish

Studs are the simplest earring style—a front decoration mounted on a post (for pierced ears) or a clip (for non-pierced ears). Drops are just a little longer—they hang just below your earlobes. Both are great for chic, small-scale style that can go anywhere. And there's a wide variety of styles—from plain to sparkly to whimsical. Choose a color that matches part of your outfit, or if your outfit is all one color, pick a strong contrast for your ears. Or go with gold or silver—they look nice with everything.

pretty and petite
Because studs are small, they never compete with the rest of your outfit— it's fine to wear a pair that glitters with casual clothes. Earlobes are different sizes, so experiment to see what size stud looks right on you.

style tip

If you want your earrings to really pop, pick a pair that contrasts with your hair color: dark earrings for blond hair or light ones for brunettes.

small and delightful

Colored drops can be a sweet surprise peeking out from under long hair. Earrings in bold colors can stand alone, so go without a necklace to draw attention to your ears.

These spiky little fuzzballs are super-light, so your lobes will be in the pink.

Pick faceted gems to set off your eyes—blue for blue or green eyes, green or amber for brown eyes.

mini-size, mega-style

Whimsical shapes show your sense of humor—here Black Kitty sports a tiny pink bow.

Every diva loves diamonds—triangle studs add a pretty sparkle to your smile.

Keep your spirits light and summery with super-cool wire-wrapped stone drops.

Hearts always say "sweet." Wear faceted drops like these for dressy dinners or parties.

Be dashing with dangles & hoops

Dangle and hoop earrings are splashy and fun. The bigger and jazzier they are, the more attention they call to themselves—and you—so wear them when you really want to show your style. They look especially cool with short hair; if your hair is long, you'll look more sophisticated in dangly earrings or big hoops if you pull your tresses back.

swing low
Pick dangles that hang freely from your ears. If they're so long they drag on your shoulders, they look silly, not cool.

style tip

If your face is round, try square or star-shaped hoops for a cool contrast.

in the loop

Round, oval, or crescent-shaped, hoops come in many sizes. A size that hangs above or below—not at—the corner of your jaw is most flattering.

Large plain hoops are the ultimate basic—here, gold ones are dressed down for everyday wear.

big on glamour

Small hoops go anywhere. Break away from the classic solid-metal version with this trendy beaded pair.

Catch the light with long, lean dangles ending in pearly pink drops.

Gypsy disks and funky beads give these chandeliers a bohemian flair.

Clips, springs & magnets

Pierced earrings look great, but not everyone has holes in her ears. If you do pierce, be sure to have it done by a professional and follow his or her instructions for keeping your holes clean until they heal. If you don't pierce, there are tons of cute options for wearing all kinds of great earring styles. Try cute magnetic studs or clip-on dangles—or any of these cool styles designed to look like the real thing, with none of the poking!

faux-pierced earrings

Magnetic charm. Hold small studs on your ears with tiny magnets placed on the back of your earlobes. The effect is totally real.

Spring into place. Hinged earrings like these hoops open so you can put them on, then close to clasp your earlobe. The hinge hardly shows.

Slide to secure. These cute hoops have pretty beads for a glam touch. They stay on with a spring-loaded clasp.

style tip

Clip-ons can slip off-center a little, so check every once in a while to make sure they're where you want them.

A design like this star-and-circles dangle is both delicate and bold.

A cascade of tiny stars brings the Milky Way right to your ears.

Eye-foolery

Your ears look pierced with clip-on dangles. They feature just enough ornament at the front of the earlobe to conceal the hinged clasp, and they're as pretty as real pierced styles.

Necklaces: short & sweet

Whether choker or chain, a short necklace can be long on style options. With a T-shirt or round neck sweater, make sure your necklace is bigger than the shirt neck and hangs easily over it. If you're wearing a blouse with a collar, put the necklace inside—you won't see as much of it, but it will make a pretty accent.

short styles

Simple beads and a bold pendant make this adjustable necklace pretty in pink.

You can never go wrong with a classic strand of pearls.

Sparkle lightly. Colored beads shine on this multi-strand choker.

The open-heart pendant lengthens the shape of this choker to make it more flattering.

high-rise
Chokers fit high on your neck, above your collarbone. They're often wider to make a big impact, like this multiple-strand suede version.

Find your ideal necklace length

What's the most flattering length for a necklace? The length that echoes the curve of your face. Here's how to find it.

1 Look in the mirror and find the widest part of your face. Trace the shape your jawline makes from that point. You can use lipstick to draw it on the mirror.

focal point

A simple strand of beads is just that much prettier with a special pendant. Some necklaces come with pendants, but you can usually add one when they don't.

2 Put on a necklace and adjust its length so it follows that line. Stand on a step stool to match the line on the mirror.

knotted cord

lobster clasp

3 Once you've found the length you like, clasp the necklace. Chain necklaces usually have an adjustable clasp so this is easy to do. To shorten a ribbon- or cord-style necklace, try tying a small knot behind your neck.

This flower pendant fills the hollow of your neck in a pretty way.

Necklaces: long & lovely

Long strands of beads make strong style accents; the chunkier they are, the more attention they grab. However, you do want to be sure that the length isn't overwhelming. Here are two good ways to make long necklaces totally wearable.

Tie a knot

Put on a very long strand of beads and tie it in a loose slip knot somewhere below your collarbone; let the rest dangle lower like a tassel. You can also try tying two strands together for a funkier, chunkier look.

Slide the knot so it sits at your ideal short necklace length to draw focus up toward your face.

Slide the knot lower on your chest so the top of the necklace makes a V—this elongates your look.

Wrap in loops

Loop a really long strand several times around your neck and adjust so each wrap sits at a different level. You can add or subtract wraps to get the best look for you.

Super-long beaded strands work well in this look. Try twisting two together to bring lots of color to your neck area.

show your colors

A silver chain with geometric silver beads reflects light onto your face. This delicate style looks striking with a simple outfit.

Gold-toned metallics shed a warm glow. The dangling disks on this pretty necklace will glimmer as you move.

Brighten up. Choose colorful beads that match or contrast with your outfit. Beads in several sizes on wire links make this strand unusual.

Style a necklace combo

Layering necklaces is one of the coolest ways to personalize your look. These combos look especially good with tops that have wide necklines or skinny straps. Plus, they're a great excuse for raiding your jewelry box! Just remember these rules of the road: Try to find pieces that have something in common, and layer them so they fall at different lengths. Got it? OK, girls—start your combos!

Layer with flair

Create a necklace combination that is right for your size—you want it to flatter your face, not outshine it. Taller girls can wear chunkier strands than shorter girls.

1 Choose one necklace to be your "foundation" and put it on. It can be colorful, quiet, or sparkly, bold or delicate, or have a pendant or locket. You can double a long necklace to be the foundation.

2 Put on other necklaces with a color or material in common with the first. If they have a similar look, your combo will look like one piece of jewelry. If not, it will look more dynamic. Both options are good.

3 Arrange the necklaces to lie smoothly, in concentric loops. If a longer one has a pendant, or if you want to tie it in a knot to give it importance, make sure it hangs free of the other necklaces.

master the mix

Cast a spell in stacked chain and leather chokers. Add a throbbing heart and dangling faux bone—way cool.

Walk the beach in strands of white and watery blue. Shell beads, knotted cord, and a palm tree design tie up a nautical theme.

Step lightly in a cascade of delicate silver chains. Arrange them so the pendants hang in order from small to large.

style tip

Your layered combo is just one part of your look. Get dressed before you put on your necklaces so you can see the full effect with your outfit.

balancing act

For the prettiest effect, mix necklaces that are slightly different in scale, like these, where the number, size, and spacing of the beads varies. The pink, white, and silver colors balance each other so none of them comes off too strong.

Earrings & necklaces for every day

When you're putting together an everyday look, don't worry about matching pieces exactly—just pair things that go with your outfit and have a similar type of look. For instance, pink goes with pink, silver goes with silver, funky goes with funky. Here are some tips to help you strike a balance that's right for you.

My face is square, so I go for longer necklaces and earrings that hang either above or below my jaw.

I like to pair V- and Y-shaped necklaces with smaller earrings— they balance each other and flatter my round face.

My oval face looks different when my hair is up, so I choose my jewelry after I do my hair.

match the proportions

To make your style look consistent, pick earrings and necklaces with the same kind of style impact. Pair delicate earrings with a delicate necklace, or match chunky with chunky—aim for similar "visual weight."

match the material

When your earrings and necklace are made with the same materials (metal, shells, glass) in the same finish (shiny or dull) they go together naturally, even if they're not really a set. The beads in these earrings match those in one of the necklaces.

Earrings & necklaces for special occasions

For dressy times, it's fun to wear sparkling, festive jewels. Just keep in mind that a little glitter next to your face has a big impact. It's easy to go overboard. When in doubt, stay on the lighter side and choose a necklace and earrings that bring out your prettiest features—your eyes and your smile.

Long-ish, sparkly earrings really dress up my heart-shaped face; I like them with short glittery necklaces.

I love to wear chandelier earrings and glittery chokers for dress-up— they're pretty with my oval face.

I like to balance my round face with long beads tied in a knot and cool cascade earrings or super rhinestone studs.

choose a hue

Pick a color theme for your necklace and earring combo—match your dress or eyes or go for your favorite tint. These clear and blue crystal beads go well with the model's blue flower hair accessory.

material theme

Rhinestones send out rays of dancing light. Try small droplets like these—at your ears and ringing the base of your neck—as a sparkling frame for your face.

I ♡ earrings!

Don't forget to:

1) Find earrings for Aunt Jane's wedding

2) Pick out jewelry for lunch with Grandma

3) Shop for a cool pair of summer earrings

4) Finish organizing earring collection!

So pretty

1

2

3

4

5

6

7

For my birthday?

The whole team should get these.

8

9

10

11

Perfect with my new dress!

13

12

14

15

16

17

Favorite necklaces

Your favorite necklace may change year by year, season by season, or even outfit by outfit, but these classic designs have a gift for style that's good for the ages. With such a wealth of pretty choices, you'll have great looks wrapped up, no matter what the occasion!

gold locket

pink pearls

side-hung heart pendant

gem chain

rhinestone pendant

beaded wire with pendant

chunky silver chain

beaded choker

colorful thread wraps

mixed glass beads

silver beads

disk pendant

colored stone pendant

string of silver stars

wooden beads

shells on knotted cord

Here a pin, there a pin

Pins are a cool and versatile way to make a simple outfit look special. They can go on the shoulder of a sweater, near the neckline of a blouse, or right below a skinny strap. A really large pin, like a fabric flower, can make a big statement on its own—but there's no rule that says you have to stop with just one!

Make a pin cluster

A grouping of pins looks great on a lapel or pocket. Start by picking a theme, like "things from the garden" or "smooth metal," then have fun finding ways to express it.

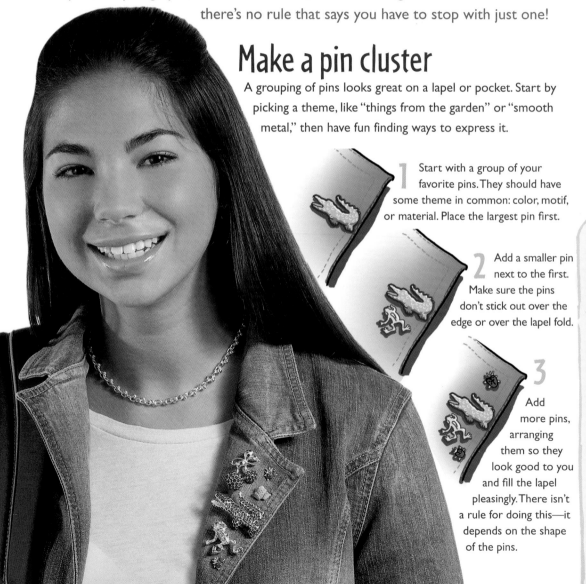

1 Start with a group of your favorite pins. They should have some theme in common: color, motif, or material. Place the largest pin first.

2 Add a smaller pin next to the first. Make sure the pins don't stick out over the edge or over the lapel fold.

3 Add more pins, arranging them so they look good to you and fill the lapel pleasingly. There isn't a rule for doing this—it depends on the shape of the pins.

style tip

Did you ever lose a pin? If you insert the prong from top to bottom, it won't fall out as easily if the clasp comes open.

Pin points

Want to make a big statement on a simple outfit? Try wrapping a ribbon or long scarf around your waist like a belt—or thread it through your belt loops—then use one big pin or a group of little ones to secure it.

Remember, the bigger the scarf, the bigger the pin should be—a tiny pin will get lost on a broad scarf.

dot them on

Flutter by—pretty insect pins are as colorful as the real thing but they hold still and won't sting!

Pin up your favorite faces with mini-portraits of movie stars, pop musicians, or favorite causes.

Glitter into style with a big brooch of faceted gemstones.

Rules of the wrist

It's temping to just throw on your favorite bracelet without even thinking—but as with any accessory, the trick to looking really polished is to work with all the other parts of your outfit. With bracelets, that means sleeves, especially. Consider these tips for getting the look right: 1) The more arm that shows, the more bracelets you can wear. 2) Shirt cuffs rule—pick bracelets big enough to fit over them or hang free of them, or small enough to slide inside them. Here are five winning combos.

with a blazer
Links, with charms if you like, are a great choice—just don't wear anything glittery unless it's a really dressy jacket.

style tip
I find it really distracting when people wear jangling bracelets in school or church or any place I need to concentrate—so I test the noise factor of my bracelets before I leave the house.

with wide or loose sleeves
Wear one big bracelet—or a cluster that looks like one. Loose bangles are good if you wear several at once.

with a jean jacket

Pick something chunky. Try a couple of big bead stretch bracelets, a cuff, or something with a big dangle. Textured materials like wood, leather, cord, or embossed metal look cool, too. Bright colors grab the eye!

with a cuffed shirt

Go with one bracelet, either tight and not bulky, like a slap, or loose enough to ride over the shirt cuff, like a bangle. To add some attitude, turn back the cuffs—you'll look sporty and the world will get a better look at your bracelets.

with short sleeves or no sleeves

Wear as many bracelets as you like, but unless you're really trying to make a statement, don't let the total get wider than the distance from your wrist to the inside base of your thumb.

Style a bracelet combo

Every time you put together a great arrangement of bracelets, you're demonstrating your fashion flair. It's all about experimenting and expressing personal style. Here are two hints to get you started: First, choose bracelets that have some common element, like color or material. Then, to judge the effect, look at yourself in a full-length mirror—this is a trick designers use to see their work from a distance, the way other people will see it.

stack them up

style tip

An otherwise simple outfit is the perfect fashion opportunity for lots of bracelets—a plain background will offset whatever you have going on around your wrists.

Rock your style with bracelets in patent leather and metallic details. This set follows a theme of pink, black, and starry motifs.

This beachy set follows a color theme closely for an overall effect that's bold but not too wild.

Ride the range with a belt-style cuff and beaded leather bangles. Desert hues set the tone and mix well with Western styles.

Mix, match, and layer

The things the bracelets are made from (glittery gems, polished stones, tumbled stones, plastic, shells, wood, leather, etc.) have as much to do with your combination's success as the type of bracelets you combine. Choose materials that together look dressy, sporty, funky, casual, or whatever expresses the style of your outfit.

1 First, gather the bracelets you want to combine. Then pick one bracelet as your base. It's easiest to begin with something big, like a set of stretch beads or skinny bangles, a slap band, or chunky beads. Put it on your wrist.

2 Add another bracelet or a set of skinny ones. Pick something that's different from the base piece but has something in common with it, too— like color or material.

3 Add one more bracelet or another set of skinny ones. Again, pick something that's different from the others but has something in common with them—or choose something in the same design but in a different color.

Keep your rings in character

What do you think about when choosing a ring to wear? Extra-large and glittery rings are real attention grabbers. They're great for fancy events—but don't forget to keep your nails nice. For everyday wear, your best bet is small rings that don't get in the way. No matter what you choose, be sure your ring reflects the person you are— or at least the person you want to be today!

what's your style?

Dreamy poet. Grace your finger with a set of several slender, muted metal bands with small stones. Faceted gems are fascinating.

Outgoing and lively. To invite conversation, wear a really big "cocktail" ring with lots of commanding sparkle.

Talented artist. Sleek sculptural shapes show your individual flare. Pick a style with a motif that reflects your take on what's truly cool.

Quiet but strong. Keep it simple— choose a delicate band with a few small stones in a plain setting.

Cool sophisticate. Slide on a set of sleek, smooth, matching bands, each set with a single small stone. Let them twist as they will.

History lover. Choose a retro or old-fashioned style. Metal with stones is romantic.

Team captain. Pick a colorful, sporty style that looks fuss-free and assertive. Stay away from faceted stones.

Head of the class. Be classic with a class ring! These rings look fancy but they're perfect to pair with school clothes or weekend wear.

style tip
Want to keep ring settings from snagging your clothes? Try painting them with clear nail polish. Check first, to be sure the ring isn't valuable.

Totally confident

A big faceted gem looks super-sophisticated. Wear this kind of ring when you want to be noticed!

A great sense of fun.
Whimsical shapes like musical instruments, animals, or insects make people smile.

Time for style

Watches are a cross between jewelry and practical gear, giving you a stylish way to keep an eye on the time. They're a lot like bracelets: Some styles are simple and pretty enough to be worn almost anywhere, but watches that are definitely sporty or especially fancy belong with the appropriate look. When you're deciding what goes with what, think about the design of the face as well as the band.

buckle up
The extra straps and hardware lend pizzazz to a classic, tailored watch.

style tip
Take a look at your watch face. If it looks scratched, you may be slamming your hands around more than you realize. Take a tip from your watch and try to be more graceful with your hands.

swing time
Charm-style watches masquerade as delicate bracelets. Choose one on a stripy pastel ribbon band for a preppy accent.

wrist wrap
Scarf-style or soft ribbon bands are certainly very girly—but how dressy they are depends on the fabric used and the style of the watch itself. Be sure to tie the knot very securely.

it's a guy thing

A big watch makes your wrist look delicate. Choose an heirloom style or something totally modern—this one has a cool spinning top with rhinstones!

watch the time

A fabric band with Velcro closure, together with a jeweled watch case creates an everyday watch with lots of sparkle.

flip top

The snap-up cover over the face of this digital ring-watch is perfect for sporty girls.

Wide leather bands like this one work best with daytime looks that are tailored, sporty, or preppy.

sweet heart

Pretty as a bracelet, this heart-shaped watch on a slender metal band is feminine but not at all fussy—wear it with jeans and tees, or with skirts and dresses.

long face

High-design types may prefer the sleek lines of a rectangular face. A colored dial keeps it from being too serious.

A watch that's meant to fit loosely (like a bracelet) with a delicate link or chain band works best when you're dressed up.

Hands-on style

You know how to choose rings, bracelets, and watches—what about putting them all together? Just remember this rule of thumb: Hand jewelry draws attention away from your face, so be conscious of how your overall look will be impacted. Ready to try your hand at an ensemble? Here are some ideas to get you started.

make an impact
Pick a chunky bracelet and watch and put them on one hand only. Make them the same color, matching a color from elsewhere in your outfit. Choose a ring with that color, too.

To keep my long fingers from looking skinny I like to wear several delicate rings on one finger.

I think my small hands look best with one delicate ring and either a watch or a bracelet, but not both.

cool combo

When you want to wear something on each wrist, choose pieces that are low-key and have something in common—like these pearly pink beads and silver watch with pink face.

Decorate your tootsies

When it's flip-flops–and-sandals weather, put on a toe ring or an ankle bracelet—or both—to jazz up your feet. The rings can go on whichever toe you like (or as many toes as you think look cool). Here are four ways to coordinate flip-flops and foot jewelry.

twinkle, twinkle
Jewel-trimmed flip-flops make feet sparkle. Let them take center stage and add delicate toe rings and anklets.

style tip
Wearing an ankle bracelet may feel weird at first. You may need to get used to wearing one.

summer blooms

Coordinates are cute. Pair a string of teeny flower beads with bold flower-trimmed flip-flops. Add matching beaded toe rings for even more flower power.

mix it up

Opposites attract—so don't be afraid to pair sturdy sandals with delicate jewels. Here a wrap-style toe ring has just the right weight, and a shimmery finish ties it all together.

gang them up

Wear a couple of anklets in the same theme. A striped canvas strap on the flip-flops calls for a casual, beachy look. How about a toe ring in the shape of a flip-flop?

Hair accessories

Heads up, girls: You put a lot of effort into looking great—don't sell you style short by just picking the first clip or ponytail elastic that comes to hand. Instead, choose your outfit and then pick hair accessories for style and color just as carefully as you do the rest of your jewelry. Whether they reinforce your look in a subtle way or steal the show with a bold piece, hair accessories truly top off your style.

smart match
Choose larger hair accessories like headbands in a style that goes with your outfit—don't mix a sparkly band with sweats! For a more low-key look, match the band to your hair color.

A comb with this much sparkle is a great way to make a simple style simply gorgeous!

Key item

To make a big style statement, use an important hair accessory like a glittery comb, big flower, or colorful bow as your primary accessory.

tress dress-up

Use twisty ponytail elastics to put the prettiest grip on long, flyaway locks. Pick colors that match your outfit. Use more than one!

Put fancy bobby pins in your hair to add surprise to a simple outfit. Even the very shortest cuts can find a spot for one or more of these.

Girls with long tresses are lucky—these hair sticks bring an exotic touch to simple updos, and keep them neat, too.

Art for your body

Temporary body jewelry is funky and fun—and best of all, you can change it whenever you're ready for a new design. There are two main types of body art: temporary tattoos and self-sticking gems. Both come in packages with suggested designs, but you can also combine them in any way that suits your fancy. Just be sure to read the packaging carefully to find out how to use them properly, and ask your parents for a thumbs-up before applying tattoos or gems.

style tip
Temporary tattoos last about a week, so check your calendar before you commit!

jewelry artist
Use temporary tattoos and self-sticking gems to create a piece of jewelry, right on your skin. Create an unusual necklace, bracelet, or cuff with temporary tattoos. Then use the gems to accent your favorite parts. Cute!

1 Cut out the tattoo and remove the plastic top sheet. Place the tattoo face down on your skin and press firmly.

2 Dip a sponge or cloth in water and rub it on the back of the tattoo until the paper backing is evenly damp.

3 Wait 30 seconds. Peel off the backing. Rinse the tattoo gently. Let it air dry.

stick them on

Glitter-and-glow cherries are perfect summertime accents.

Choose exotic curled shapes or fancy butterfly outlines in black for a bohemian effect.

Let a school of colorful dolphins swim around your ankle or down your arm.

mix and match

Use a mix of body gems and temporary tattoos to decorate your upper arm, your calf, or any other spot large enough to feature more than one motif.

Treasures for hands & feet

If you were stranded on a fashioable desert island,
which accessories would you need? Whatever your
treasured pieces are, they're bound to attract
attetion. Whether you go funky, dressy, casual,
or just everyday cool, pick bracelets and
watches thoughtfully to complement your outfit
and your personal style.

1 multi-strand
bracelet
2 glam watch
3 beaded stretch bracelets
4 silver bangle
5 funky bead bracelet
6 pretty shell bracelet
7 classic pearl bracelet
8 pink gem ring
9 dangly cherries toe ring
10 filigree ring
11 brown beaded toe ring
12 blue beaded ring
13 funky plastic ring
14 dolphin ring
15 double-band ring
16 feather butterfly ring
17 silver butterfly ring
18 beaded toe ring
19 dangling disk anklet
20 pearl-and-stars anklet
21 glass bead anklet
22 turquoise cuff watch
23 square silver cuff watch
24 cute polka-dot watch
25 ribbon-strap watch
26 brown bead anklet
27 knotted cord bead anklet

Spice it up

Give a surprise finish to your style by adding a pretty hair ornament, a cool body jewel, or a super pin. To see things on the back of your hairdo, face away from a big mirror and look into a hand-held mirror.

1 Decorative bobby pins, hair pins, and mini-barrettes make hairdos shine with style.

2 A twist-in flower makes a subtle centerpiece for updos.

3 This rhinestone sparkler looks pretty on all hair types.

4 Plastic mini-jawclips are casual favorites.

5 Shiny metallic mini-clips dress up or down with ease.

6 Hair sticks and vertical clips hold a hair twist with flair.

7 Square barrettes have the coolest edge.

8 Bright flower bobby pins are super-festive!

9 This funny fuzzy pin makes a statement.

10 With jade-colored petals, this flower pin looks smart.

11 This pin has feathers and gems and beads—oh my!

12 This chic square pin gives bird-lovers a good name.

13 A jeweled dragonfly looks classic on a lapel.

14 This beachy flower pin is at home on a summery outfit.

15 Tiny earrings can double as pins.

16 Body gems are gorgeous!

17 Temporary tattoos are even cooler in a sparkly finish.

Nierah

Rosie

Amy

Alexis

Nikki

Pick the pieces that tie your look together

Bags, hats, scarves, belts, gloves, and sunglasses are great style changers. When you wear them, you're not only styling an outfit, you're doing what fashion pros call "extending your wardrobe." Since they help give basic clothes different looks, these accessories are a great way to refresh a favorite ensemble or polish the look of special outfits. So how do they work for you? Do you wear a variety of styles or stick with a few that give you a signature look? Do you like to make a big statement or use accessories to tie together your look in subtle ways? Whatever your style, this section will help you make the right accessories choices for you.

Put big bags to work

When you've got lots to carry, stash it in a large bag. Generous backpacks, shoulder bags, and large totes are the bags to choose when you're carrying a big load. Pick the type that works best for each purpose—messenger bags can be a nice change from a backpack for school books or sports gear, and a compact backpack may work just as well for shopping at the mall (think hands-free) as it will on a hike in the woods.

style tip

When you're wearing a big backpack or shoulder bag you need to pay attention to who or what's behind you—you don't want to bump a wide load into your friends.

stash and carry

Tote-style shoulder bags are easy to get things in and out of. And things that don't fit exactly (like an umbrella) look OK sticking out of the top. If you stash lots in a soft tote, check the mirror for bulges that look messy. And keep in mind—totes don't offer much security from prying hands or the weather, so pick one with an inside zipper pocket for your wallet.

pick your style!

Make a splash—watery blues send this stripy tote to beach, pool, or anywhere else you want to look and feel cool.

Take a stroll—straw is perfect for summer outings. Leather trim and flower appliqués are sweetly sassy.

Carry a "conversation" print—pick a tote patterned with things you love, like these shoes and bags.

Wide straps keep you comfy when you're carrying a big bag—especially when it's filled to the brim.

the big easy

A big tailored shoulder bag is more sophisticated and not as bulky as a backpack, and you can get lots into it. This kind of bag is great for papers and notepads and things you want to keep flat. Piped pockets with grommets and D-rings add pizzazz to this purple corduroy example.

Small bags travel light

You'll always look pulled together if you pare your carry-along gear to the minimum essentials so it fits in a smallish bag. There are two basic types of small bags: shoulder bags and handbags. Choose a small shoulder bag when you want your hands to be free. If you go for a handbag (short straps or no straps) you'll have to hold on to it or put it down somewhere.

style tip
Try tying the straps of a small shoulder bag in a bow to turn it into a handbag.

sleek sophisticate
Small shoulder bags are neater than big ones, and still give you hands-free carrying. Leather in a pretty color with a flap-and-buckle closure is right for almost any occasion.

get a grip

Hit your stride with a small zip-top shoulder bag—star-trimmed leather pairs well with both jeans and skirts.

Bright clutches like this pink-and-green daisy design work great alone or can be slipped into larger bags as organizers.

Tiny beaded styles are sophisticated—great for times when you really want to dress up.

neat and trim

For a classic, pulled-together but casual look, choose a cloth handbag with outside pockets. Tweedy fabric trimmed with a bow is super-chic.

Clip on a fancy key ring for added fun.

Pick brims for sunny days

Brimmed hats have lots of character. When you're choosing one, tilt it at several angles to see the effect and try your hair different ways, too. Consider the season you plan to wear it, too: Brimmed hats in straw or canvas are perfect for sunny days. For winter, wool or felt versions are best—they'll help keep the heat in and keep the snow out of your face.

on or off the range
Cowgirl hats are fun to wear; they can be tilted to the side, the brims can be rolled, and they come in lots of colors and materials. Jeans and tees are an obvious match for a cowgirl hat, but tiered skirts look pretty cool, too.

style tip

It's almost always considered polite to remove your hat indoors.

pick your style

A bucket hat shades your eyes. Cute versions like this are great for boating, walking, or hanging out.

This wide-brimmed hat has a tallish crown (the top part) and a splashy '60s print for fun.

A really wide floppy brim like this one is perfect for reading in the sun.

classy classic

A sleek cloche, with a small down-turned brim that flares ever so slightly, takes its name from the French word for bell. Wear this style pulled almost straight on your head, not tilted too far to the back or the side.

Caps for all seasons

Caps—brimless styles and those with bills or earflaps—can be cool and cozy. There are funky styles with attitude, styles that keep you warm, and others that shield your eyes from the sun. Even if you think they absolutely "make" your outfit, most caps should be taken off indoors—the exception is a summery one that's knit or crochet, which you can leave on all the time. Arrange or tilt your cap to find the angle you like best.

totally tops

Newsboy caps come in different proportions. Test them to see whether you like the bigger or smaller scale best.

Some knit caps cover your ears and others don't. Pull them down on your forehead, then experiment to choose a straight or curved line above your eyes.

LOVE

Baseball caps are always fun, and a great way to keep the sun off your face.

snow cozy

Snuggly warm insulated caps—the kind with a cuff and earflaps—tend to make your head look bigger. Don't fight it. Just play along and choose one that's colorful or has cute details like pom-pom ties.

crafty stuff

Handmade looks are cool for caps. Whether crochet, like this one, or knit, colorful yarns make you smile at winter gloom.

style tip

Wear a hat you feel comfortable in—if it makes you feel stylish, you'll communicate confidence. If it makes you feel silly, go without.

Trim it up

You probably don't change your bag every day, so it makes sense to choose one that really reflects your style. And then why not add a flourish to personalize it, either to match an outfit or keep it distinct from other girls' similar bags? You can add jewelry, a scarf, some ribbon, or, if you like to do crafty projects, you could add painted designs or cool appliqués (ask an adult first if that's OK). Here are some ideas to try.

A big fabric flower pin looks especially nice on a fabric bag. Pull from the same color family as your bag for a soft look.

Make your bag special

There are lots of ways to add pizzazz to a bag. Cloth and straw bags are easier to embellish than leather or plastic ones, because you can pin into them without hurting them—but you can safely tie things onto the handle of any bag.

1 First, look at your jewelry and scarf collection to see what would make a cool accent. Pick pieces that look good with your bag and each other.

Show off a favorite pin by placing it prominently on your bag. This sparkly pin really catches your eye.

awesome accents

This polished stone pin has the sophisticated look of jade in a playful design.

This scarf has silver threading to add interest and a touch of shine to your bag.

A colorful butterfly pin looks pretty perched on a bag or a shoulder.

A square pin can be centered on a pocket to look like part of the original bag design.

2 Add your accent choices: Tie a scarf around the handle. You can also place a pin on the pocket, flap—or both.

A silky scarf tied onto the bottom of a strap looks casually elegant. Double it up for a shorter, pouffier look.

Pick sunglasses with flair

Your choice: Make a big statement with big glasses, or be more low-key. If you're picking small glasses, shapes that make a contrasting angle on your face are a sure bet, but frames that repeat your face shape show lots of attitude. Or try on the biggest pair you can find—it's fun when glasses dominate your face. You can also try colors that match or contrast with your hair, or choose colors that match your outfit.

style tip

If your hair is long enough for a ponytail, try on sunglasses with your hair both loose and pulled back to find a versatile pair.

fly away

Aviator glasses (like these, with two bars across the bridge of your nose) suggest adventure. Cool candy colors make them girly. Check different pairs to find your best look—shapes vary.

the look

Wraparound glasses cup the side of your face and hide more of your eyes. The ones shown here are rimless, but you'll find plenty with pretty and colorful rims, too.

Cat's-eye frames have a slanted, almond shape that makes most wearers look cool and sophisticated. The eyes on some pairs are more exaggerated than the eyes on others.

Go glam. Movie-stars-to-be will get a boost from retro styles worn by divas of the past. These slightly chunky, squarish shapes look great paired with ponytails or head scarves.

square off

Square frames look cool on almost everyone. Try on slender wire frames as well as thicker plastic ones to see which scale looks best. Go for a bright color to make a strong statement!

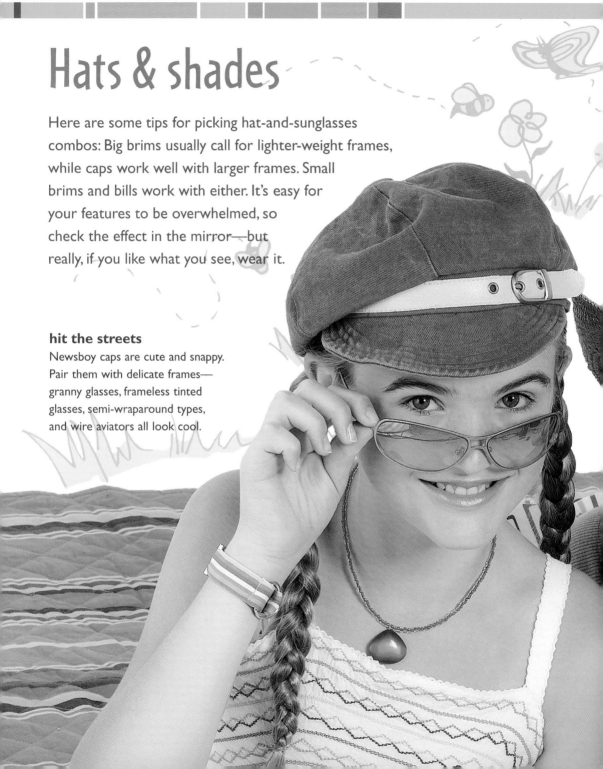

Hats & shades

Here are some tips for picking hat-and-sunglasses combos: Big brims usually call for lighter-weight frames, while caps work well with larger frames. Small brims and bills work with either. It's easy for your features to be overwhelmed, so check the effect in the mirror—but really, if you like what you see, wear it.

hit the streets
Newsboy caps are cute and snappy. Pair them with delicate frames— granny glasses, frameless tinted glasses, semi-wraparound types, and wire aviators all look cool.

A small-brimmed hat and delicate cat's-eye frames look best on my round face.

My face is square so I go for diagonals— angled brims and upswept frames.

Wider brims and frames keep my oval face from looking long. I'm cool in most large frames.

To contrast the top of my heart-shape face, I tilt my hats and wear small frames.

take the reins

Cowgirl and other big hats have lots of style. Wear them with quieter frames that are not too decorated, like wraparounds or understated classic oval shapes. Stay away from aviator or cat's-eye frames—they have so much style they'll compete with the hat.

Scarves go the extra fashion mile

Long scarves have tremendous personality, which they'll happily
lend to whatever outfit you wear them with. Tie them on your head,
around your neck, around your waist and hips—different fabrics give
different effects, so be creative. Use a bright or patterned scarf to
jazz up a plain top, or a plain scarf to tone down a busy outfit.
You can never have too many scarves!

Heads-up on scarves

A classic way to wear a long scarf is wrapped around your
head. This flattering style frames your face in a pretty way
while it keeps hair back. It can be tricky to get the knot and
placement right, so ask a friend for help if you need to.

1 With hair pulled back out of the way,
wrap a long scarf around your head like
a headband. Place it over or under your ears
as suits your look. If the scarf is too wide,
fold it or pleat it to make it narrower.

2 Tie the ends together in a
knot with streaming tails.
Experiment to see if you like
the tails at the base of your
neck or above or below one
ear. Then fix your hair in a
ponytail or let it hang loose.

Easy does it

Breezy cotton stripes make a cool head wrap that looks sleek with the ends hidden under your hair. But for fun, rotate the scarf and tie the ends in a perky bow at your temple.

style tip

Wearing a scarf with a necklace is too much—it overwhelms your face. Unless you choose a really simple necklace, it looks better if you wear a scarf alone.

This scarf comes rigged to be a headband—with a built-in elastic, tying the ends is just for decoration.

Buckle up

Belts do more than hold your clothes close to your body. They can accent or minimize your waistline, fool the eye into thinking your torso is longer than it is, and add a cool fashion accent to your outfit. If your clothes have belt loops, it's usually best to pass the belt through them, but if you're wearing a top or dress with no obvious waistline, you have more options for placing the belt.

it's a cinch

Sling low. Braided leather makes a belt both flexible and chic—great to drape over your hips.

This cool fabric belt looks like a necktie. The metal D-ring fastener is a casual touch.

A pretty scarf like this one can always double as a belt. Just pass it through the belt loops of your favorite jeans. Crisp fabric will tie in a perky bow, too.

A buckle is like jewelry—key the buckle style (not just the belt color) to your outfit.

style tip

If you don't want to call attention to your waistline, choose a belt that matches the color of your outfit. The buckle should be the same color or have a dull rather than shiny surface.

pull it together

Thread a sturdy belt through belt loops when your top is tucked into your jeans. When your top is outside your jeans, anchor it with a wide or double belt or another interesting style. Tie a pretty woven string belt like a sash over pants without belt loops.

Try wrapping a ribbon or long scarf around your waist like a belt—or thread it through your belt loops—then use one big pin or a group of little ones to secure it.

Go hand-in-glove

Most gloves are worn for a specific purpose—to keep your hands warm—but that doesn't mean they can't be stylish. Whether you're looking for gloves or mittens, take along the coat, jacket, or sweater you'll wear with them so you can choose the right color and style. There is a wide range of style options available, from funky to fun to sweet and even frilly.

pick a pair

Insulated gloves—in tailored-leather or sporty styles—protect from snow and frigid weather.

Cozy knit and crochet gloves with pretty trims have a sweet, retro appeal.

Fingerless gloves keep your hands warm and leave your fingertips fully functional.

Short cotton gloves with contrasting fingertips are cool and definitely eye-catching.

Wrist warmers are funky and let you show some attitude—they're definitely not for dress-up.

graceful glamour

Satin gloves are super-dressy—for weddings, formal dances, and other very fancy events. White and off-white are good choices for any outfit; or if you're lucky, you may find a pair in the same color as your outfit. Most styles you'll find will be stretchy.

style tip

For gloves, short nails are best—long or broken nails can be uncomfortable and can damage your gloves.

D-ring belt

Style to go

Belts, bags, and gloves are important accessories that work hard for you—to secure your jeans, warm your hands, carry your gear. But you choose them as much for the way they look as for the way they'll do their job. When shopping for new pieces, ask yourself these questions: Does it go with something in your closet? Is it suitable for the time and place you'll wear it? Is it in scale with your size? Do you love it? If you answer "yes" to all four, you may have found a keeper!

Quilted evening bag

Western belt

Sporty clutch

Satin stretch gloves

Tailored handbag

Long wrist warmers

Retro knit gloves

Leather flower-link belt

Beaded tie belt

Sporty backpack

Satin handbag

Fingerless gloves

Canvas handbag

Patterned shoulder bag

Sequined tote bag

Ribbon belt

Top off your look

Scarves, hats, caps, and sunglasses can change the look of
an outfit—and that's what makes them fun to choose and
wear. They can compliment or change the look of your face
too, so look in the mirror and let yourself
be whoever you see if you like the way
she looks. Here are some favorite styles.

1

2

3

4

5

6

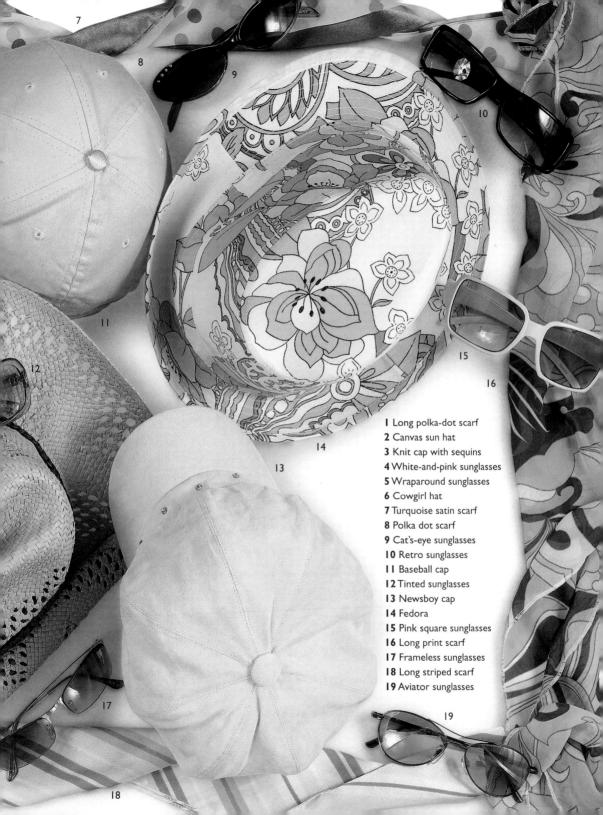

1 Long polka-dot scarf
2 Canvas sun hat
3 Knit cap with sequins
4 White-and-pink sunglasses
5 Wraparound sunglasses
6 Cowgirl hat
7 Turquoise satin scarf
8 Polka dot scarf
9 Cat's-eye sunglasses
10 Retro sunglasses
11 Baseball cap
12 Tinted sunglasses
13 Newsboy cap
14 Fedora
15 Pink square sunglasses
16 Long print scarf
17 Frameless sunglasses
18 Long striped scarf
19 Aviator sunglasses

Must-have accessories

Whatever your look is, whichever style is your favorite—or at least your favorite for today—there are certain accessories you can count on to make you look and feel stylish, and you'll always want to have them in your closet. You might choose something with a different style or color than the examples shown here, but with these ten terrific accessories on hand, you're set to be super-chic.

1

Big hoops. Simple and classic, plain hoop earrings like these provide a pretty accent that looks great with casual, sporty, and semi-dressy clothes. Plus, they're nicely low-key and at the same time big enough to show under longer hair.

2

Super shades. Sunglasses make big statements—pick a pair with the shape, color, size, and personality to match your style.

3

Best bag. Tote your stuff neatly and easily, but with distinction. A sporty style like this keeps you ready for action.

4

Cool watch. Be prompt and pretty with a colorful wristwatch. To avoid the straight and narrow, pick one with interesting strap details and a bold face.

5

Chain bracelet. A loose chain bracelet is incredibly versatile and goes with all but the dressiest clothes in your closet. Choose one like this classic with heart-shaped charm, or pick a different kind of dangle or locket ornament that broadcasts your own style.

6

Bold headband. Wide headbands are so super-cool, short-haired girls will want to go long. You can find headbands in bright or quiet colors, big or small patterns, and even in different textures, so there's one that's just right for each of your favorite outfits.

7

Multi-strand bracelet. Delicate but big enough to have character, a multi-strand bracelet adds a grown-up flourish to your wrist.

8

Lovely locket. A long, delicate chain necklace with a locket looks sweet and lets you keep a photo or other special little keepsake close—it's fun to open the locket and show your friends what's inside.

9

Fabulous flip-flops. Make them pretty enough to wear on the street—with a big flower or another cool accent—and in a color you simply love.

10

Super studs. Small earrings are simply perfect for anywhere and anyone. Every girl needs a glittery pair—and a simpler set, too.

Rosie

Nierah

Alexis

Nikki

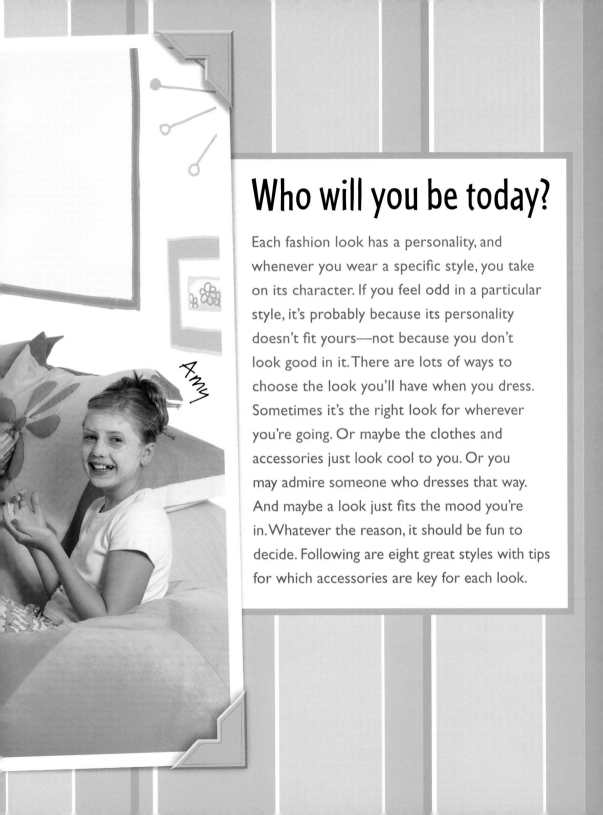

Who will you be today?

Each fashion look has a personality, and whenever you wear a specific style, you take on its character. If you feel odd in a particular style, it's probably because its personality doesn't fit yours—not because you don't look good in it. There are lots of ways to choose the look you'll have when you dress. Sometimes it's the right look for wherever you're going. Or maybe the clothes and accessories just look cool to you. Or you may admire someone who dresses that way. And maybe a look just fits the mood you're in. Whatever the reason, it should be fun to decide. Following are eight great styles with tips for which accessories are key for each look.

Bohemian chic

Be a free spirit with a very definite sense of style, and take your inspiration from the hippie looks of the 1960s. Go for natural materials—like stone beads, leather, and feathers—and artsy details.

Short beaded-dangle necklace

Small, rimless or granny-style tinted sunglasses

Feather earrings

Crinkly scarf with glittery accents

Tumbled-stone and glass-bead bracelet sets

Textured leather thong sandals

Wild western

Show your love of the wild, wild West with leather, silver, and turquoise and coral accents.

Dangly silver-and-turquoise earrings

Crushable woven straw cowgirl hat

Turquoise medallion on beaded choker

Leather cuff with stone-and-silver medallion

Leather belt with silver conchas and buckle

Glam diva

Lavender and rhinestones—what could be nicer? Indulge your eye for satin, feathers, and glittery trim. Go easy though, so you look dressed up—not like you're playing dress-up.

Cat's-eye sunglasses with rosy lenses

Small rhinestone choker

Satin handbag with gemstone key chain

Super-cool boa, made of fabric or feathers

Surfer girl

So you love the beach and
endless sunshine, island prints,
shell beads, and sea-swept
hues? Dress yourself in things
that capture the spirit of waves,
breeze, and palm trees—cool
bright colors, lots of little beads,
and waterproof everything.

Tropical-print
bandanna

Aviator shades—
tinted blue

Short, summery shell-
bead necklace

Ankle bracelet and
matching toe ring

Sand- and ocean-
colored bead bracelets

True romantic

Soft pretty accessories, just a touch of glitter, a string of pearls—these are staples for a classic, romantic style. Girls who feel at home in this look love bows and subtle colors, and they don't think twice about wearing frilly accents with their sweater sets—or with jeans and tees, either.

Chiffon scarf

Sweet pearl or silvery bead choker

Pretty watch with ribbon band

Pink-glass bead bracelets

Delicate filigree ring

Star athlete

If you live for sports, pick accessories that can take a bit of action. Go for fun colors, tough materials, and graphic details like blocky numerals or soccer balls. Don't forget to take off jewelry before you hit the court of take to the field!

Leather choker with basketball bead

Colorful backpack with soccer motifs and charms

Necklace with player number dangle

Bright ankle socks with basketball pom-poms

Urban legend

Stroll the streets and visit cafés wearing tough but pretty black and silver accessories. Choose things that are small overall—but just a bit bulky and edgy too, with metal studs and buckles and a bit of sheen and sparkle. Crochet caps look great— and you can keep them on indoors.

Crochet cap with scattered sequin accents

Sophisticated square sunglasses with smoky lenses

Chunky chain necklace with dangle

Small handbag with pink die key ring

Silver bangles, plain and twisted

Debutante

If your social scene has you mixing, meeting, and greeting, you want to look poised, calm, and totally collected. Pick accessories that are ladylike and not too frilly—your look stems from the 1950s and '60s.

Sleek, square retro sunglasses

Big, floppy fabric-flower pin

Long silky scarf, striped or geometric

Classic watch with colored face

Pretty pearl-trimmed headband

glossary

Accessories: Wearable items other than clothes

Bangles: Bracelets without clasps, loose enough to slide on over your hands

Bill: The stiff oval piece that extends over your forehead on a baseball or newsboy cap

Brim: The part of a hat that flares out around your head; it may be large or small, turned up or flared down

Brooch: A large, decorative pin

Cap: A small hat. This word is used for brimless styles, styles with fold-up cuffs, and styles with bills.

Chandelier earrings: Long earrings that have several tiers of dangling elements

Charm: A small ornament, which often hangs from a bracelet

Chic: Fashionably stylish (this is the French word for style)

Choker: A tight necklace that sits above your collarbone

Crown: The part of a hat that sits over the top of your head, above the brim

Dangles: Hanging earrings more than one-inch (5-cm) long

Designer: A person who comes up with ideas for accessories, garments, fabrics, or other fashion items and oversees their creation

Diva: A star or leading lady; a glamorous style (this is the Greek word for goddess)

Drops: Hanging earrings less than one-inch (5-cm) long

Ethnic: With style characteristics of a specific culture; usually used to refer to traditional but non-Western fashions or design elements

Hoops: Wire ring earrings; they may be round, oval, crescent, and even square; they sometimes have beads or other ornamentation

Hue: Another word for color

Locket: A hinged pendant that opens to hold a small photo or other keepsake

Look: A combination of clothing and accessories that have particular design features; a specific fashion style

Pendant: A piece of jewelry that hangs from the center of a necklace

Proportion: Size or dimension, usually used to compare one element to another

Scale: Same as proportion

Studs: This word has several meanings in fashion: 1) Small earrings that sit on your earlobes, without hanging elements 2) easily removable, non-sewn buttons used for men's formal shirts (the kind worn with a tuxedo). 3) Small metal ornaments affixed to clothing or jewelry, usually in a decorative pattern.

Style: 1) When used as a noun or adjective, this word can mean a specific fashion look or a flair for putting looks together. 2) It can also mean the particular way something is designed, for instance, bell-bottom and boot-cut are two pant leg styles. 3) When used as a verb, style means to select and pull-together the pieces of a fashion look or to design individual accessories, garments, fabrics, or other fashion items.

Stylish: Having style; usually—but not always—meaning something is currently fashionable

Stylist: A person who selects and pulls together the pieces of a fashion look (usually for photography or television) or who works with a designer to develop the design of individual pieces

Trend: A popular fashion style; trend is usually used to identify or forecast a change in what is fashionable

index

Acknowledgments

The publisher would like to thank the following for their kind cooperation in the preparation and production of this book:

Our fabulous models: Sakura Akiyama-Bowden, Brittany Barbone, Andrea Bloom, Tess Brokaw, Amy Cacciatore, Alexis Carmody, Michelle Chionchio, Mary-Kate Duffy, Kelsey Evenson, Rosie Fodera, Hannah Gross, Nierah Jinwright, Sade Johnson, Maghee Kelsall, Sade Johnson, Juliette Lam, Nikki Lam, Francesca Lobbe, Juliana Merola, Kristin Molinari, and Autumn Stiles…and also their parents, who stuck with us so very patiently at the photo shoot.

The amazing hairstylists: Azad Desmeropian, Shukran Dogan, Catherine McDermott, Rhondalyn Roberts, John Lisa, and Angela Woodley, for their wonderful skill and dedication.

The super stylists: Maria Stefania Vavylopoulou and Shima Green, for outfitting the girls in the coolest clothes.

Special thanks to Vincent DeRosa and Suzanne Humbert at Whisper Soft Mills for the beautiful bedding and furnishings.

Thanks also to Josephine and Katherine Yam and the team at Colourscan for their hard work in bringing it all together; to Nanette Cardon for her work on the index; and of course to the always-glamorous Angela Coppola, Donna Mancini, Cristina Clemente, Nichole Morford, Sharon Lucas, and Gregor Hall for all their help and support.

Hair products used in this book included these products from the L'Oréal Studio Line: Crystal Wax, Out of Bed Whipped Gel, Mega Mousse, Mega Gel, Fast Forward, and Finishing Spray.